AMERICAN GOODS

AMERICAN GOODS

A COLLECTION OF ESSAYS ON LAW, ECONOMICS, SPORTS, NOSTALGIA, AND PUBLIC INTEREST

Bruce J. Cooke

To order additional copies of this book, contact:
Xlibris
844-714-8691
www.Xlibris.com
Orders@Xlibris.com
817605

Contents

Dedication Page

This book is dedicated to several people for their love and support. It is dedicated to my parents Victor and Margaret and to my brother Cookie. It is also dedicated to my Uncle Andy, Uncle Eddie, and Aunt Mae who lived upstairs from me and helped raise me along with my parents and brother.

It is also dedicated to five teachers who inspired me to achieve and enjoy my educational journey; Mr. Velebir and Mr. Geydoshek in Columbus. No. 8 School, Mrs. McGowan in Garfield High School and Dr. Bednar and Dr. Voyatsis in Muhlenberg College.

It is also dedicated to my wonderful cat Victoria who I had for fourteen years and is now in cat heaven.

Preface

I am fortunate to have several passions in my life. I have been a huge sports fan ever since I was six years old when I listened to the 1958 World Series on my parents' old Dumont radio. While growing up in Garfield, New Jersey, I learned to like school. I became a school addict, not only getting an MBA, but also a law degree.

This book of essays is about law, economics, sports and nostalgia/public interest. These essays are intended to help people understand in simple language information on law, economics, and sports. This book is also about nostalgia and how the present and future can be as good as the best year of your life.

Readers could use the information in this book in several ways. They could use this information to start planning their estates and to learn how different areas of the legal system operate. The section on economics explores how different concepts interplay in the economy. In the appendix, I have provided a listing of all amendments to the US Constitution and an economic history of the United States. Finally, for baseball fans, I have provided a list of the ten greatest achievements by players in one season as determined by an ESPN survey.

Acknowledgments

The author graciously acknowledges the contributions of the following sources in the compilation of this book.

Outside Sources

- Mercer County, New Jersey State Bar Association
- Nolo Press, San Francisco, California
- US Department of the Treasury
- *Law Dictionary*, Barron's Educational Series, Steven Gils, editor
- *Beyond Basketball*, Mike Krzyzewski with Jamie K. Spatola, Warner Business Books, 2006
- *The Great Crash-1929, John Kenneth Galbraith*, Houghton Mifflin Company,1997
- *The Law of Schools, Students, and Teachers in a Nutshell* (2nd ed.1995)

Main Legal Cases/Laws/Codes

- New Jersey Administrative Code, section 10
- 42 US Code 1396
- US Constitution, Amendment I
- US Constitution, Amendment IV

- *Lemon v. Kurtzman* (Supreme Court, 1971)
- *Elk Grove United School District et al. v. Newton et al.* (Supreme Court, 2004)
- *Tinker v. Des Moines Independent Community School District* (Supreme Court, 1969)
- *Bethel School District No. 403 v. Fraser* (Supreme Court, 1986)
- *Thomas v. Board of Ed. Granville Cent. Sch. Dist.* (607 F. 2nd 1043).
- *New Jersey v. TLO* (Supreme Court, 1981)

Introduction to Legal Essays

I enjoy writing about subjects that I have studied. I like to write essays about specific topics that provide useful information to people in an understandable format. It is my wish that the collection of the following essays on law will shed some light on common topics for those who have never studied these subjects.

The legal section of this book is designed to give the layman an overview of important situations that most people will encounter in everyday life. Each separate essay will give one a summary of a particular legal topic. The essays are in an easy-to-understand language, without the complicated legal jargon that one often encounters in legal books.

The legal essays do not generally address any particular individual situation. However, the essays give the practical aspects of each concept and enable one to make a judgment as to whether professional legal advice is required.

The legal essays are as follows:

- "Legal System and Courts Overview"
- "Estate Planning"

- "Estate Administration"
- "Real Estate"
- "Small Business"
- "Elder Law/Medicaid Eligibility"
- "Education Law"
- "Federal Feeding Programs

The courts overview reviews the function of lawyers and the purpose of each type of court normally found in a state. "Estate Planning" reviews what one needs to know about planning one's estate and the smooth transfer of wealth. "Estate Administration" concerns a step-by-step process on how to administer an estate after a loved one has passed on.

The "Real Estate" section leads one through the issues that one faces in renting an apartment and buying and selling real estate. The "Small Business" section gives one an orientation into the choice of legal entities that a small business owner has in structuring her business. The "Medicaid Eligibility" section summarizes the rules one encounters when contemplating putting someone in a nursing home in the state of New Jersey.

The "Education Law" section gives a summary of First and Fourth Amendment issues in the school setting. The Federal Feeding Program essay gives you an introduction into available feeding programs of the Federal Government.

Courts and the Legal System

There are a large number of courts and tribunals in any state. This essay will give one a summary of the various courts and administrative tribunals that handle different types of legal matters.

Criminal Courts

Given the exploits of Perry Mason and Marsha Clark, the most well-known courts are the criminal courts. Criminal laws are different in every state. They are defined as crimes against the public, rather than an individual. Serious criminal violations such as murder, rape, and kidnapping are defined as felonies and are punishable by death or imprisonment of more than one year. Less serious violations such as shoplifting, trespassing, and traffic offenses are usually punishable just by fines.

The procedure in criminal cases begins with the grand jury. First of all, a group of people is brought together to see if there is adequate evidence for the state to bring charges against a defendant. If the case goes to trial, a unanimous jury must decide beyond a reasonable doubt that the defendant is guilty. If guilty, the defendant is sentenced by the judge. The sentence is determined by statute, but the judge usually has some discretion in sentencing. The guilty party is then sent to jail for the prescribed time unless a successful appeal occurs.

Civil Courts

A civil court is where one goes to settle a private dispute. This private dispute can involve many things, including a contract dispute, a motor vehicle accident, an assault, etc. Sometimes, a private dispute is decided before a judge and sometimes before a jury. The standard of proof is less than that required in a criminal trial. In addition, if the case is decided before a jury, only a majority vote is required for a successful action.

If one is awarded a money judgment in a civil court, the next step is to collect the amount due. First of all, you have to find out where the defendant has her assets. This involves finding out not only the city where the assets are located but also whether they are in a bank, a mutual fund, or real estate. Once this information is collected, papers can be filed with the proprietors of the assets, and transfers to accounts can usually be worked out to satisfy the judgments.

Special Civil Courts

There are several types of special civil courts to handle specialized functions. Among these courts are family courts, surrogate courts, and small claims courts. Family courts handle divorces, separations, adoptions, etc. In short, any matter concerning the fixing of rights and responsibilities of married persons vis-à-vis each other and their children is handled by A Family Court.

Surrogate courts handle the registration and interpretation of wills, trusts, and the administration of estates. Most of these actions are straightforward, but there are occasional disputes in this area. Disputes may involve undue influence or an unclear intention of the testator.

There are two special courts that usually handle small claims and where individuals frequently represent themselves. Disputes of a private wrong, called a tort, or a contract nature involving less than $2,000 can be handled in the small claims court. Disputes concerning back rent or apartment damage are handled in landlord/tenant court. If you are handling your own case, make sure to take pictures or other evidence to court.

Estate Planning

Estate planning enables you to plan your estate and helps ease the burden on loved ones after you are gone. When serious illness strikes, a power of attorney and a living will ease the stress of the burden of caring for a loved one. When the end comes, an improperly planned estate can be very stressful to your survivors. They not only have to deal with their grief, but also with the many details involved in the disposition of an estate. A properly executed letter of instruction takes care of many of the details of the estate. Finally, if you do not have a will, your estate is distributed according to the intestacy laws of the state and not your wishes.

A power of attorney enables your loved ones to act on your assets while you are incapacitated. It is an instrument that can be revoked at any time. Most individuals have at least some of their assets in their own names. In case of serious illness, your loved ones may need to use some of your assets immediately. With a properly executed power of attorney, someone can withdraw money from your bank account while you are laid up in the hospital. A power of attorney can be executed for a specific purpose, such as to take money out of the bank, or can be in general for all actions that the principal would take, including buying and selling real estate.

After you return to health, you can revoke the power of attorney. This option is useful as affections toward certain individuals frequently change. For instance, you may have given your spouse a general power of attorney and suddenly you become estranged and want to separate from him or her. If you did not have the option of revoking the power of attorney, you would be left in the situation of having a person who you no longer care for having full power over your assets.

A living will or advanced directive allows you to control what types of artificial feeding or equipment will be used to keep you alive when you are in a partial or total vegetative state. This document informs the appropriate health-care authority that you do not wish to be kept alive by artificial means but wish to die naturally. This document also gives you the right to designate someone to act for you in deciding whether you are to be kept alive by artificial means in a given situation and you are unable to act.

When death occurs, the first task involves planning the funeral or cremation. A properly executed letter of instruction informs the executor what the deceased wanted in terms of a funeral. This eliminates the need for shopping around for a funeral home at a time when an individual is suffering the ultimate stress of the loss of a loved one. Moreover, further stress may be added by the fact that the individual planning the funeral may not know what the deceased wanted in terms of last wishes . . .

Estate Administration

When a loved one dies, it is necessary to provide for an orderly estate administration process. The goal of estate administration is to identify assets, to collect assets, and to distribute them as best as possible according to the intent of the deceased. You also have to wind up the deceased's affairs, which involves notifying offices like social security and filing necessary tax returns. If you are a detail-oriented person and not too bereaved, you can handle estate administration yourself. The following essay will give you an idea as to what is involved.

Identification of Assets

The identification of assets can be easy or difficult depending upon two things. First, if the deceased was somewhat wealthy or had an interest in a lot of assets, it may be difficult to create a complete listing. Second, if the deceased never made a list of his assets or talked about them, it may be very difficult to create an accurate listing. It is very helpful when the deceased creates a document called a letter of instruction, which not only identifies assets but also gives burial wishes among other things.

Assets are generally classified as liquid or nonliquid. Assets can also be owned jointly or solely. Liquid assets are those that can be turned into money immediately, such as checking accounts, savings accounts, and cash on hand. Nonliquid assets are those for which you must follow more formal procedures before obtaining value. These assets include real property, pensions, stocks, automobiles, and social security benefits.

If the deceased owned an asset jointly with someone, that asset becomes the property of the co-owner without a legal process. For instance, your mother passes away and one of her bankbooks was listed as "either Mary Smith or her daughter, Jane Smith." The money in that account becomes Jane's by merely going to the bank with a copy of the death certificate. No other legal process is required.

Administration Process

The process of estate administration follows a timeline. The important thing to remember with every activity concerning the deceased is to keep copies of all bills. First, keep a record of all unpaid bills of the deceased, including medical bills, and pay all valid bills. Second, keep records of all burial, cremation, memorial services charges, etc. Next, obtain as many copies of the death certificate as you can. The funeral director usually gets the death certificates for the family. Now, you are ready to move the deceased's assets to an estate account and begin paying bills. After the bills are paid, you can make distributions, file any necessary tax returns, and close the estate.

Real Estate

Most people are involved in one or more of the following real estate transactions one or more times in their lives:

- Rental of an apartment or house/condo/coop
- Purchase of a condo, coop, or house
- Sale of a condo, coop, or house

Real estate transactions are important for two reasons. First of all, the cost of housing is getting higher every day. They are not making any more land. Only a certain number of residential houses are available wherever you live. If you rent a facility, you want to make sure that you are getting good value for your dollar.

Second, you want a facility that is safe and warm. Housing needs are recognized as the second most important human need after food and water.

Following is a list of important things to look for when you are involved in various types of real estate transactions.

1. Rental of a Residence

When you first leave home, one's first experience with real estate transactions is usually as a rental of an apartment or house. If you are renting an apartment from a commercial source, you will be required to sign a lease. Apartment leases are usually contracts of adhesion. That means you must accept all the provisions, or you won't be accepted by the landlord.

Make sure you read the whole lease and can live with all the provisions of the lease before signing it. *If* you don't like what is in the lease, you can always shop around. You will also probably be asked to provide security. Security is usually one month's payment of rent upfront that the landlord holds until you leave the residence. Make sure that you check the duration of the lease, provisions for canceling the lease, and how you must return the residence in order to get your security money back.

When you rent a living facility from a private owner, you have some additional concerns. If you are going to live with a stranger, it is important to find out as much as you can about your future housemate for safety purposes and for compatibility purposes. If the owner is not asking you to sign a lease, you better be sure what the understanding is as to leaving—how much notice do you need, and how much notice does your landlord expect? You need to find out if your housemate smokes, drinks, stays up late, etc. What are the cooking and cleaning arrangements? Can you have company over? Can the company stay overnight?

2. Purchase of a Coop/Condo/House

For most people, buying a home is the most significant purchase one makes in life. There are many factors to be considered, including location, cost, style, future use, property taxes, and schools. The concept of location includes if it is in a flood zone, in a high-noise area, in a safe area, and the quality and proximity of schools. Cost involves whether one can afford the down payment and mortgage loan on the house. Style involves size, number of bedrooms, bathrooms, and aesthetic quality of the house. Future use means if it is going to have enough rooms to accommodate a growing family as well as future resale value. Property taxes are used to pay for schools. One needs to determine if the property taxes can be afforded and if the schools are of a high-enough quality.

It is a good idea to utilize both a realtor and an attorney when purchasing a home. You could look at houses on the Internet, but a realtor gives you personal service that you can't get from a computer. A realtor has knowledge of the available homes in the area and has probably visited many of them. The realtor fee is usually paid by the seller, so you don't have to worry about an additional up-front payment.

An attorney helps a purchaser in several ways. First of all, an attorney is able to review the contract of sale more thoroughly than a layperson can. An attorney looks for any hidden clauses that may be detrimental to a purchaser, such as assurance that the land is not in a flood zone. The attorney for the buyer supervises the home inspection process to make sure all repairs before closing are performed in conformance with the contract and to the buyer's satisfaction. The attorney also checks title and arranges for title insurance. If you are purchasing a coop, your purchase must be approved by the coop association. An attorney would negotiate the mechanics for such an approval.

3. Sale of a Residence

When you are selling a residence, your most important goal is to obtain a fair price and a ready buyer in a certain time frame. If you know a lot about the real estate market in your area, and the market is really hot, you may not need a realtor. However, in most situations, a realtor is a necessity. Realtors commonly charge a commission of 3 percent to 6 percent. For this fee, they perform two essential functions. First of all, they tell you the value of your house, and they tell you what to fix up to maximize the value of your house. Second, they list your house in a register, and they show your house to interested parties. When they find a buyer for you, they also provide a standard real estate contract.

Closing of a Sale

The closing is the most important part of the purchase or sale of real estate. It is the point where the transfer of legal ownership of the property takes place. By this time, the buyer's attorney has checked the chain of ownership for the property. The buyer has inspected the premises. The bank has approved the mortgage for the transaction. The attorney for the seller prepares the deed. She checks that any problem with the premises has been corrected, there are no impediments to the chain or ownership; the bank has approved the mortgage, and the deed is in proper form. Everything must be ready to go.

At the closing, the buyer's attorney acts as the closing agent and prepares the RESPA statement. This is a complicated spreadsheet that accounts for all utility, tax, assessment, inspection, and all other fees. The closing attorney credits and charges the buyer and seller as the situation warrants. The closing agent also distributes checks as warranted. The seller's attorney checks the RESPA and deed to make sure that his client's interests are protected. If everything is okay, the deed is transferred, checks are transferred, and the keys are given to the buyer.

Small Business

President Calvin Coolidge once said that the business of America is business. Many people have their own business, and the legal system recognizes different business structures. These structures govern the relationships of the business to employees, customers, and third parties. Depending upon individual circumstances, one must decide how to legally structure a business. The different types of arrangements are sole proprietorship, partnership, corporation, and limited liability company.

Sole proprietorship is the simplest type of business structure. This type of structure is most advantageous for the small family business that does not have to worry too much about raising a lot of capital and being held liable for accidents that may happen on the premises. This structure gives the owner the most control and requires the least paperwork. All revenues and expenses are noted on the owner's individual tax return. There is no double taxation. The main disadvantages are a limited ability to raise additional capital and unlimited personal liability if someone should fall on the premises or be damaged in some other way by the business.

A partnership type of business arrangement is ideal if you and another want to have equal say in the running of a business. Before you start, partners must agree on several things, including the percent of ownership of each partner, management, size of the business, and hiring and firing authority of employees. You can set up a limited partnership where one partner is not involved in running the business but invests in the business and shares in profits. There is no double taxation in a partnership. Profits are divided according to the partnership agreement. A major drawback to a partnership is unlimited personal liability of all managing partners.

Corporations

Incorporation offers several advantages to the new businessman or businesswoman. There is great prestige in being called president of your company. In addition, the corporate form offers tax advantages, continuity of existence, and limited personal liability. Corporate officers can also write off health insurance costs.

Without a corporate form, the personal assets of a businesswoman can be reached for debts of her company. For example, if a customer slips on the sidewalk while visiting a manicurist, the manicurist can be liable from her personal assets for the injury suffered by the customer. Someone could break their neck and sue for $750,000. If the insurance only covers $500,000 and there is only $100,000 in assets in the company, the manicurist could lose her life savings of $150,000. She could have been saving her money for her retirement or her children's college education.

If the manicurist had her company incorporated, the customer's recovery would have been limited to the amount of the insurance plus any assets in the company or $500,000 plus $100,000 or $600,000. The personal assets of the manicurist would have been protected. The customer would not have been able to pierce the corporate veil, and the manicurist's life savings would have been protected.

The disadvantages of incorporating, which are corporate taxes, registration fees, and excess paperwork, are minor compared to the advantages of limited liability and tax savings. In addition, if a sole proprietor has less than 35 employees in her company, she can file as an S corporation. Owners in this corporate form are not liable for corporate taxes. Even as a C corporation, a middle-class sole proprietor should be able to write off most, if not all, income as salaries. New Jersey has a small yearly registration fee which all corporations must pay but can be recouped in tax savings.

In addition to the liability protection and potential tax savings, there is prestige in being the head of your own company. The end of the year is the best time to incorporate because you can start a fresh set of accounting records for the new year. In addition, if you want to register as an S corporation, you need to do so by March 15.

Limited Liability Companies

The limited liability company has become a favored business form for many individuals. This form offers companies the protection of limited personal liability without the possibility of double taxation of profits. Profits and responsibility are structured according to the limited liability agreement. The disadvantage of this form is that states treat LLCs differently and constructing the operating agreement is often cumbersome. Case law on limited liability companies is relatively new, so you can't really be sure how disputes are going to come out.

Medicaid Eligibility

When you or a loved one enters their golden years, there is frequently a need to qualify for Medicaid benefits in nursing homes.

Medicaid is a federal and state medical assistance program, which will pay nursing home and medical costs for eligible individuals. To qualify for Medicaid benefits, an individual cannot have more than $2,000 or $4,000 in assets depending on monthly income. If your assets are too high, you have to spend down your assets to the amount that qualifies you for Medicaid benefits. If you have $70,000 in assets and are in the $4,000 category, you must spend down $66,000 in assets before you are eligible for Medicaid ($70,000 − $66,000 = $4,000).

The financial situation of the Medicaid applicant is carefully reviewed to see if there has been any improper transfer of assets prior to the date that the Medicaid application was submitted. This is known as the look-back period. Since February 8, 2006, the look-back period is sixty months. Any transfers made prior to February 8, 2006, will continue to be subject to only a thirty-six-month look-back period. Certain transfers would not be deemed improper.

However, the Medicaid applicant's money can be used to purchase some items for fair market value for the benefit of the applicant. The individual's assets can be used to purchase items, such as haircuts, manicures, pedicures, a television, and a radio. The Medicaid applicant's assets can also be used to purchase a burial space, a prepaid burial, or an irrevocable burial trust for the Medicaid applicant. Transfers for the benefit of a community spouse or a blind or disabled child are exempt from the penalty period.

A transfer of the principal residence is treated like any other resource. However, a transfer of the principal residence will not trigger a penalty period if it is made toward the following: (1) the community spouse; (2) a child who is under twenty-one, blind, or disabled; (3) a child who has been residing in the residence for at least two years and provided care for the parent that allowed the parent to stay home ("caretaker child"); or (4) a sibling who also has an ownership interest in the residence and has resided in the house for at least one year and otherwise meets the eligibility criteria.

In conclusion, there are basic asset and income requirements for Medicaid eligibility. If you meet both criteria, you can get a free ride on Medicaid in a nursing home. However, if you have transferred certain assets within a look-back period, you are ineligible for Medicaid for the penalty period and must private-pay for the amount of time that you are not eligible.

Student Rights in the Public Schools

Introduction

There has been a great amount of interest in the news lately about the rights of students in public schools. Without proper control in the classroom and in the school, it is impossible for students to learn. Sometimes, the need for control in the school collides with the rights of students under the Constitution. Rights of students under the Constitution are not absolute just like the rights of all citizens are not absolute. For instance, we have no right to yell *fire* in a crowded theater.

First Amendment

First Amendment issues concern applications of the Establishment Clause and Free Exercise of Religion Clause of the First Amendment. It also concerns general student speech in schools.

Establishment Clause

The Supreme Court elucidated a three-part test in determining whether a school action violated the Establishment Clause in *Lemon v. Kurtzman*. The standard reads as follows: "(1)Legislation or government action must not have a religious purpose; (2) Legislation or government action must not have the primary effect of either enhancing or inhibiting religion; and (3) Legislation or government action must not create excessive entanglement between church and state."

A recent well-known Establishment Clause case was *Elk Grove United States District et al. v. Newton et al.* (Supreme Court, 2004). An atheist Newdow filed an action for his daughter alleging that the words "under God" in the Pledge of Allegiance constituted violations of the Establishment Clause and Free Exercise Clause of the First Amendment. The two issues for the court were whether Newdow had standing to sue for his daughter and whether the First Amendment was violated. The Supreme Court ruled that Newdow did not have standing to sue for his daughter.

Concerning the First Amendment issue, several concurring opinions held that the Pledge of Allegiance did not violate the First Amendment. Justice O'Connor wrote that the Pledge of Allegiance was not unconstitutional because the challenge was on only two words in the pledge and one can avoid saying "under God" and still meaningfully participate in the exercise.

Free Exercise of Religion

The first immigrants came to this country seeking religious freedom. The Constitution protects the free exercise of one's religion and prohibits the state from establishing a preference for one religion. Regarding the Free Exercise Clause, the Supreme Court has distinguished between the freedom of individual beliefs, which are absolute, and the freedom of individual conduct, which is not. The Free Exercise Clause protects an individual from certain forms of government compulsion; it does not afford an individual a right to dictate the conduct of government's internal procedures.

Beliefs must be accommodated, but accommodation of certain conduct may encroach on others' religious beliefs. The Free Exercise Clause is violated when one is compelled to perform an act that violates one's religious beliefs or forgoes a benefit bestowed by the government.

First Amendment Free Speech

The Supreme Court Case *Tinker v. Des Moines* held that students do have free speech rights in schools as long as the school cannot prove a reasonable forecast of school disruption.

Courts balance the interests of student rights with the school's need for order when assessing a student's free-speech claim and the threat of school disruption. Courts have distinguished the school's need for order based on whether the disruption was on school grounds and/or involved school activities. Where a middle school student went to school with a T-shirt emblazoned with the words "Drugs Suck," the court found that speech need not be sexual to be prohibited by school officials. The conviction of students for a sit-in at school was upheld where certain students assembled on school grounds outside the principal's office. According to the court, the principal "had the right and duty to take reasonable measures to restore order."

At the same time, student speech has been upheld where the prohibitions were outside of school grounds. In *Thomas v. Board of Ed. Granville Cent. Sch. Dist.*, students in a junior-senior high school published a satire entitled *Hard Times.* They printed and distributed the publication outside school grounds. School officials found the publication offensive and potentially highly disruptive. They suspended the students for a full five days. The Court of Appeals ruled for the students in an obvious large sarcastic statement for free speech. "It is conceivable that school officials could consign a student to a segregated study hall because he and a classmate watched an X-rated film on his living room color television."

For all those who say that Supreme Court justice and New Jersey's own Samuel Alito is too conservative, recent decision shows his propensity to uphold the rights of students' free speech. In July 2004, the Third Circuit

Court ruled that a Pennsylvania law prohibiting student newspapers from running their ads for alcohol was unconstitutional. At issue was an act that denied student newspapers advertising revenue from alcohol beverage ads. Judge Alito wrote, "If government were free to suppress disfavored speech by preventing potential speakers from being paid, there would be not much left of the First Amendment."

Fourth Amendment—Protection from Unreasonable Searches and Seizures

Teachers and principals have frequently found it necessary to search students and remove items that may be harmful to them and to others. The prevalence of drugs, bombs, and mass murderers has broadened the importance of school searches to include offenses that may subject the student to criminal prosecution. The courts have ruled that students have a right to privacy that is protected by the Fourth Amendment and this right cannot be invaded unless the intrusion can be justified in terms of the school's legitimate interests.

Student Searches: Existing Supreme Court Standard—Reasonableness/ Intrusiveness

In *New Jersey v. TLO*, the Supreme Court held that the Fourth Amendment applies to schools, and in order for searches to be constitutionally valid, reasonableness must prevail. "The legality of the search of a student should depend on the reasonableness, under all circumstances, of the search." Reasonableness of a search comes into play at two levels. The first level involves the following question: was the motivation for the search reasonable in light of the information obtained by the school official? The second question involves the reasonableness of the search itself. The search must be reasonably related to the object of the search and not excessively intrusive in light of the age and sex of the student and the nature of the infraction.

This Supreme Court standard has not been overturned and has been interpreted by lower courts in numerous situations. In one case, a teacher observed one of her students uncharacteristically talkative with glassy red eyes. The student asked to get a drink of water, but upon leaving the classroom, she turned in a direction opposite of the water fountain. The teacher thought she was under the influence of drugs and reported the matter to the principal.

The school tested the student for drugs and alcohol and searched her locker. The tests were negative and no illegal drugs were found. The girl's father sued the school, alleging that his daughter was subject to an intrusive search, including the testing of bodily fluids, without reasonable suspicion in violation of the constitutional protections against unreasonable search and seizure under the Fourth Amendment. The Third Circuit ruled for the school, holding that the symptoms that the student possessed created a reasonable suspicion that she had consumed some quantity of alcohol or other drugs.

New Jersey courts have overwhelmingly upheld student searches as reasonable. A student having a bag, together with a prior incident involving student's possession of a burned marijuana cigarette, justified the search of a student's knapsack. A search was upheld where a confidential informant told school officials that a fellow student was dealing drugs on school premises. A search of the student's hand luggage carried on field trips was upheld as reasonably related to the school district's duty to provide discipline.

Blood testing is permitted even when less-intrusive means of ascertaining whether a student has consumed alcohol are available. However, where schools have attempted to justify searches on less-than-reasonable suspicion, the searches have been held to violate the constitutional rights of students. (Policy requiring drug and alcohol testing of all students suspended for fighting held unconstitutional.)

Federal Feeding Programs For You And Me

There are Federal Feeding Programs out there for you, me, our parents, and our kids. Among these programs are the WIC program, the SNAP (Food Stamp Program) the Child Nutrition Programs (Child Care, School Lunch, Summer Lunch, Senior Lunch) and the Food Distribution Program. No one should go hungry in this country. Famous people have enrolled in these programs. There is no stigma involved. You paid taxes for these programs. You are entitled to them. Application information for all these programs is available online.

SNAP-Food Stamp Program

The Food Stamp (SNAP) Program is for individuals separately and families alike. There is an income test and resource test for eligibility. Once eligible, you are given a debit card to use at USDA Authorized stores. You take this card to stores and shop for eligible foods including dairy, fruits and vegetables, breads/rice/ cereals and meat/poultry and fish. You can also use your card for water, soda, snacks and cakes. However, you cannot redeem benefits on your card for non-food items like liquor, vitamins or flowers.

Child Care Program

The Child and Adult Care Programs have various aspects. There is a School Lunch and Child Care Feeding Program for students in pre-school and schools as well as regular year-round programs. There is also a Summer Lunch Program. Schools and Non-Profit Organizations file applications online for approval. Once approved, they get reimbursed for the meals they serve. If they serve meals in poor areas, they get a larger reimbursement. There is also an Adult Care Feeding program for senior adults.

WIC

The Special Supplemental Nutrition Program for Women, Infants, and Children (WIC) provides federal grants to states for supplemental foods, health care referrals, and nutrition education for low-income pregnant, breast feeding, and non-breastfeeding postpartum women. The program is also for infants and children up to age five who are found to be at nutritional risk.

Food Distribution Programs

The *Food Distribution Program* strengthens the nutritional safety net through the distribution of USDA Foods and other nutrition assistance to children, low-income families, individuals in emergencies, Indian reservations, and elderly individuals. Among the programs are the following.

The Commodity Supplemental Food Program (CSFP) works to improve the health of low-income pregnant women, new mothers, infants, children, and the elderly by supplementing their diets with nutritious USDA Foods.

The *Food Aid Program* provides U.S. agricultural commodities to feed millions of hungry people in needy countries. through direct donations and concessional *programs*.

The *Food Distribution Disaster Assistance Program* supplies USDA Foods to disaster relief organizations such as the Red Cross and the Salvation Army for mass feeding or household distribution.

Introduction to Economics/ Accounting Essays

Economics is called the dismal science. People think that it is just a collection of statistics with no relationship to people or everyday events. On the contrary, everything that happens in the economy is related to everyone and everything that happens in the world. Economics is a living, breathing social science that connects an ever-changing world with how people earn their living, where they live, and what must be done to adapt to changes in the world.

These essays will attempt to explain some common economic terms and principles by using everyday language and easy-to-understand examples.

Essays will be presented on the following topics:

1. Money
2. Banking
3. Inflation and Recession
4. Prime Interest Rate
5. Stock Market
6. Stock Market Crash of 1929
7. Budgeting

The section on money will explore the origins of money as a means of facilitating trade and establishing the price of things. The essay on banking will explain the function of banks as a means of safeguarding money, expanding the money supply, and creating wealth. The sections on inflation and recession explain how the economy can get out of balance via excessive demand with inflation or how it stagnates via a recession.

The next section explains how the Federal Reserve bank expands and contracts the money supply by manipulation of the prime interest rate. The next section is on the stock market. There is also an essay on the Stock Market Crash of 1929. The final section is on budgeting and how to adjust budgets as life changes occur.

Money

Ever since the beginning, man has struggled with the environment in an effort to stay alive. The earliest man would either grow or kill what they needed to survive. They killed animals and used the hide to keep warm in the winter. As time went on and civilization advanced, it was found to be more efficient to trade some of the value created. If a person was a good hunter, he would trade his animal skins for the food he needed.

As societies and communities developed, money started being used to expedite trade. Eric may want spices from India but only had deer hides to trade. The spice salesman may not want the deer hides. However, if Eric could sell his hides to someone else and get some money for them, he was in luck. He could use this money to pay for the spices, as long as the spice salesman accepted the money. The earliest forms of money were tokens and coins.

The United States makes just enough money to provide for an efficient economy. Money must be backed up by some value, or else it is meaningless and inflation develops. To have an orderly economy, a given amount of money must indicate a certain value, or else a country could not survive and chaos would develop. A structured exchange system makes possible expectations about what people need to have in order to satisfy their needs and wants.

If a train trip no longer costs $10 and no one knew what it costs, there could be no travel, and inertia would develop. There would be no transactions and no employee wages. You couldn't hire anyone because you wouldn't know what to pay them. If you were a small businessman and sold widgets, people wouldn't know how much to pay for your item. You wouldn't sell anything and wouldn't make any money. Even if you had money and went to buy food, the market wouldn't know what to charge you, and chaos would develop. There are many factors that go into the value of goods and services. Suffice it to say, money is necessary for an orderly economy.

In the modern computer world, there are many different types of money. Besides cash, there are checks, credit cards, and ATM cards. Checks are used for the convenience of payment. It is not efficient for the electric company for you to pay your electric bill with cash when there are a million people paying a fee every month. It is much more convenient and easier to compute if you pay by check. Payment by check entails the electric company sending your paper check to a bank, where the bank credits the electric company and debits the payer or individual paying the bill's account.

Credit cards and debit cards are electronic methods of payment. Credit cards involve a company, such as VISA, giving you a sum of funds, you can draw upon and then pay back at given intervals. Debit cards include funds that you already have on deposit, say, $1,000. If you want to buy a suit for $200, the salesman slides your card and you now have $800 on deposit.

Banking System

The first goal of a banking system is to provide a secure place for citizens to store their money. If the money was lost or stolen, as in the Old West, many people lost their life savings as deposits were not guaranteed. Most deposits today are backed up by the Full Faith and Credit of the US government.

A second function is to provide for a more efficient means of trade. This is done via the check system. For example, if Jack has at least $100 in his account at bank A, he can pay his $100 electric bill by writing a check on his account at the bank. He sends this check to the electric company, which takes the check to their bank B. The electric company's account is credited for the $100. This bank then sends the check for payment to bank A. This bank takes $100 out of Jack's account and sends a $100 credit to bank B. As you can see, it is a lot easier to pay by check than for Jack to have to travel a hundred miles to pay his electric bill.

A third function of a banking system is to provide an orderly means for the expansion of the economy. This is accomplished via the legal reserve requirement. When people put their money into banks, they naturally have a right to take out these funds anytime they want to. However, this by itself does not provide for any growth in the economy. If Mary wants to start a business that will create jobs, she needs money. This capital comes from banks that will loan her the money, assuming they feel Mary can pay back the loan.

A bank can lend her money that was deposited by others because of the legal reserve requirement system. The legal reserve ratio is usually 20 percent. This means that if there is $1,000,000 deposited in bank A, a bank cannot lend out $200,000 in deposits. (20 percent of $1,000,000) but they can lend out $800,000. This system is based on the belief that individuals will keep most of their money in the bank. They will not make a run on the banks as it so happened in the Great Depression. The main reason for this is that the FDIC of the federal government insures deposits up to $100,000.

By giving Mary her loan, the bank has increased the money supply and expanded the economy. Mary can take this money and hire workers, thereby creating jobs. She can also deposit some of this money in another bank B. This new bank B can take Mary's deposit and lend out a percentage of it, thereby expanding the economy even more. This creates a ripple effect throughout the economy. Unfortunately, sometimes the economy expands too fast and inflation develops.

Inflation and Recession

Inflation

Inflation is an increase in the volume of money and credit relative to available goods, resulting in a substantial and continuing rise in the price level.

As noted above, when money is lent out by a bank, there are more funds available to an investor. This increase in the volume of money can be used to pay workers additional wages. These increased wages put additional money into the economy. With this additional money, there is increased demand for the available goods and services in the economy. This causes the price of available goods to eventually rise. This is so because the amount of goods supplied at the given price level does not automatically increase with added demand. It takes time for the market to adjust.

This concept can be explained via the use of an example. The price of any good is determined by the intersection of its demand and supply curve. It is common sense that more of a product will be demanded at a lower price than at a higher price. You can sell more DVD's at $100 than you could at $200. Likewise, the public will demand more DVD's at $100 each than at $200 each. Let's say the point where demand equals supply is at a price of $130.

If more money and credit are pumped into the economy, inflation will cause the price level to rise. Let's say there are 1 million DVD's being bought and sold every month at a price of $130. If more money is pumped into the economy via loans and other means, people who would not buy DVD's before now have the money to buy DVD's. This increases the demand for DVD's. Given the constant supply of the product, this pushes the equilibrium price up to $150 and inflation develops.

Recession

If the price level and demand fall too much, a recession may occur. A recession is a time of reduced economic activity. The official definition is two consecutive quarters of negative growth. When a recession occurs, unemployment increases because there is too little investment in the economy and too little job creation.

A leading cause of recession is lack of confidence in the economy. When people feel that the chance of succeeding in a new business venture is poor, they won't borrow money to invest because they don't want to lose their hard-earned savings. Without new investment, no new jobs are created, new housing does not get built, and the economy stagnates.

This lack of confidence in the economy causes the stock market to drop. A tax cut can be passed to try to spur the economy. Without proper government controls, a depression similar to what happened in 1929 could occur.

Neither inflation nor recession is good for the economy. When the Fed sees a threat of either one of these phenomena, they will institute some fiscal policy by manipulating the interest rate.

Prime Interest Rate

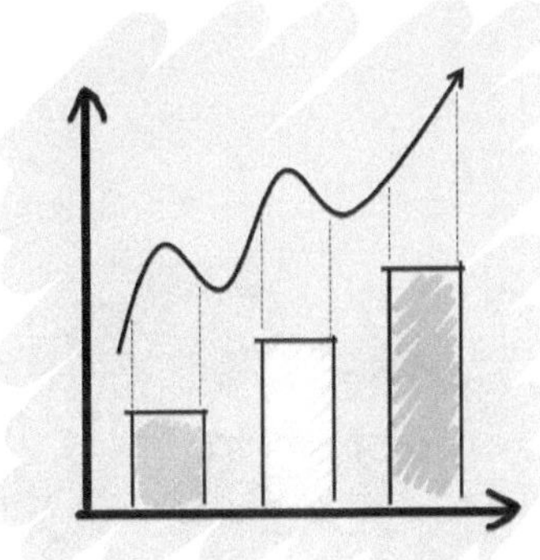

When the economy is expanding too much, the price level for products and wages rises too fast. This makes for an unhealthy situation for everyone. What we can buy before with our wages is no longer available to us. When the price level rises too fast, the Federal Reserve bank tries to reduce inflation by increasing the prime interest rate, thereby reducing demand for loans throughout the economy. The prime interest rate is the loan rate that the Fed charges to member banks to borrow funds.

If the Fed increases the loan rate for member banks, there is less incentive for banks to borrow money from the Fed to lend out to customers. This causes a reduction in the demand for borrowed funds because the bank is now charging an increased interest rate to customers. For example, if the Fed charges 5 percent for a loan of 1 million, the bank has to charge 5.5 percent on its loans in order to make money. At this higher rate of interest, fewer loans are demanded, less money goes into the economy, and there is less demand for products and the price level drops.

Stock Market

Everyone who works for a living either works for the government, for themselves, or for someone else. As you are well aware, the government gets their resources from various tax measures. You and your employer obtain resources from selling a product or a service or a combination of both. Most small businesses obtain the money they need for starting up from their own resources or from private bank loans.

However, a large number of businesses, especially big businesses, need large amounts of capital. They obtain this capital by selling shares of the company on what is known as the stock market. As an incentive to get individuals to buy these shares, companies may offer dividends. A dividend is a distribution of profits or earnings to shareholders at stated periods. The amount any stockholder receives depends on if they own common or preferred stock.

Shares of stock of these publicly traded companies are bought and sold in the stock market. The stock market in the United States reflects the confidence that people have in the future profitability of these companies and, therefore, in the economy as a whole. A stock such as Microsoft may be selling for $100 per share. Yet if people think that the company has a bright future, they may bid $110 per share on the stock to induce current owners to part with their shares. If the stock is now being traded for $110, people who bought the stock for $100 have made 10 percent on their investment in addition to the dividends that they are receiving.

Confidence in the economy can be affected by many factors. Most notable are earnings reports of large companies and housing start-ups. If large companies are not doing well and new housing is not being built, fear develops that the companies may lose money or may not be able to grow. This causes people to start selling their stock. This pushes the price down as people will accept a lower price per share than what they initially invested.

A vicious cycle occurs, the price of other stocks may go down, and unemployment occurs. This is what happens in a recession. Fortunately, there are government controls in place to keep a recession from escalating into a depression. The Federal Reserve will pump money into the stock market to keep it from going too low. This tends to help employment and lead the economy back on the right track.

Stock Market Crash of 1929

After WW1, business was booming in the country and the Roaring twenties ushered in unparalleled optimism. As President Coolidge said "The business of America is business." With this optimism, the stock market went up and up. Unfortunately,

this changed fast in 1929. The market spiraled down with panic selling and no one knew how to stop it. Misery ensued for millions as they lost money, jobs, and homes.

Much has been written about the causes of the Stock market Crash. The economist John Kenneth Galbraith offered his ideas about the causes:

- *Favorable Trade Balance- Unlike today, we had a very favorable trade balance in the 1920's. Countries owed us monies from WW1. We increased tariffs on imports to collect part of the money owed as other countries started paying up. The problem was American exports fell especially for the farmers. They could not sell their products abroad.*
- *The banking structure was inherently weak. There were a large number of independent banks who could not survive a run on their deposits. With banks failing, there was minimal money for new investment in the economy.*
- *The bad distribution of personal income. The economy was highly dependent upon the rich buying luxuries and investing in new ventures. When the economy started going bad, the rich pulled back on their spending.*

There are now strict controls in the market to prevent future crashes. Among them are detailed requirements for companies listed on the exchange and automatic stoppages in trading if there is too much selling in one day.

Budgets and Budgeting

Budgets are helpful at all stages of life because everyone needs money. A high school or college student may live at home, but she needs money for a car, clothes, and extracurricular activities. A young man may have to plan for commuting expenses on a job, as well as for clothes and activities. If one marries, has children, and buys a house, a budget is important to keep up with mortgage payments and saving for college. Budgets are helpful for senior citizens because they live on a fixed income.

In conclusion, a person who has a budget has control of his finances and knows what he can and cannot buy. This gives one peace of mind. A wise person once said, "To have a happy life, live below your means."

In any kind of managed activity involving the use of resources, it is helpful to estimate financial activity in order to compose your budget and maximize your resources.

This estimation often itemized is a listing of expected revenues and expected expenses during a given time period. When one plans activities to reach a goal, one also has to plan costs and how to meet them, A realistic goal requires the use of a budget to ensure that adequate resources are available to meet the goal.

To make the best use of a budget, actual revenues and expenses need to be compared with the budget as the budgeted time period transpires. If revenues are higher than expected, you have a nice problem. You can spend money on something that you did not expect to be able to fund. If expenses are higher than expected, you need to cut back mid-stream on one of your activities. For example, if you were paying for tennis lessons for your son and daughter at $1000 each and you are short $1000, you have to cut back on half the lessons.

An Excel budget program is helpful to plug in changes in expenses as life situations change. Such a program helps you match expenses with revenues. Just create a spreadsheet with these headings and some simple commands. Multiply daily times 30 to get monthly expense totals. Multiply weekly times 4.1 to get monthly expense totals.

ITEM	DAILY	WEEKLY	MONTHLY
FOOD	30		900
CLOTHES		6.2	25
CAR PAYMENT/CAR SERVICE			50
CHILD CARE		6	25
MEDICAL			10
MORTGAGE/taxes			75
AMUSEMENTS			15
OTHER			

TOTAL------ 1100

If you have upcoming changes in revenues or expenses, always check the impact on your taxes of these changes. If the change is going to increase your taxes like more revenue, you need to look for ways to minimize the change. If the change is going to decrease your taxes like adding another dependent, make sure your tax return reflects such a change.

Introduction to Sports Essays

There have been many changes in sports in the past forty years in all areas of the sporting world. Some of the changes have been good, such as the increased participation of international athletes in professional sports. Also, the increased opportunities for female athletes in all areas have enriched the sporting world for all of us. The many new opportunities for handicapped athletes to participate in sports is not only a plus for the sporting world, but it is also a credit to our society.

At the same time, there have been some disturbing changes in sports. Children who used to have the summer off now feel pressured into SAT and sports camps. The result in many cases is anxiety that leads to nothing but failure. The levels of obesity among children are disturbing. Fortunately, the sports world is trying to combat that trend. The NFL's Play 60 program is a prime example of a great program addressing the problem.

Participation and interest in sports are a good thing as long as we keep everything in balance. Physical activity is good at any age without regard to results. Wholesome enthusiasm as a player or a fan leads to meaningful interest in events that can be transformed into other areas of life as well.

Sports Essays

- Jimmy Connors
- "Women and Handicapped Athletes"
- "College Sports"
- "Steroids"
- "Great Sports Role Models"

Jimmy Connors

The best thing about playing sports is when you play with love of the game or enthusiasm. There is no one who has played with more enthusiasm than Jimmy Connors has. Tennis is one of my favorite sports, along with baseball and football. I became a big tennis fan when I was at college in 1973. It is no coincidence that this was when Jimmy Connors rose to prominence in the sporting scene.

Connors was not the greatest tennis player although he was a great player. Federer, Borg and Sampras won more grand slams. Not all his antics were commendable, like when he would grab his crotch. However, he was the most entertaining to watch and interview. He brought a fire to the game in the 1970s that increased interest in tennis tremendously. He brought all sports fans into tennis. Sports fans saw him as a fighter and as macho. Working-class baseball and football fans who thought tennis was a sissy sport liked Connors. He was one of them.

Jimmy Connors had a profound effect on tennis in the United States. Arguably, he had as big an effect on tennis as Babe Ruth had on baseball and Muhammad Ali had on boxing. He transcended the sport because he expanded the popularity of the sport to bring in non–tennis fans, and the best American players have tried to copy him. For his big matches at the US Open, Jimmy would go in with an entourage. He was Ali going in for a heavyweight fight. Jimmy always knew what to say to the media to increase the interest for a match.

A few present-day players, including Novak Djokovic and Serena Williams have copied his enthusiasm, as exemplified by the fist pumping and rapport with the crowd. As attractive as these players are to see, none of them do it as well as Jimbo did. Most players today are just in tennis to make a living. They don't exhibit a true love of the game and the fight like Connors did. The fans recognized this trait in Connors and they loved him for it, especially in New York City and at the US Open.

Between 1974 and 1991, Jimmy Connors was the US Open. He achieved unparalleled success at the US Open. He won five championships. He was the only player to win the US Open on three surfaces- clay, hard courts, and grass. Connors was never number one in the world after 1982, but he was always competitive at the US Open. He made at least the quarterfinals in sixteen out of eighteen years, and one year he was injured.

The crowd roared for Connors in New York at a different level than it did for other players. He was able to elevate his game with the roar of the crowd and his fist pumping and his never-say-die attitude. After 1982, the fans sensed that McEnroe, Lendl, Agassi, and Sampras were better players. However, they knew heart when they saw it. Connors's old coach, Pancho Segura, always said Jimmy had the heart of a lion. He was their guy. As Mike Lupica of the *Daily News* wrote, "When Connors won, it was like the home team won. Everyone went home happy."

Any tennis fan who followed the 1991 US Open will remember it forever. Even though he didn't win the championship, many people consider it the highlight of Jimmy Connors's career. People remember it as Connors' Open. Only hard-core fans remember that Stefan Edberg actually won the tournament. The statistics will show that a thirty-nine-year-old tennis player ranked in the mid-hundreds reached the semifinal of the US Open. However, the excitement, joy, and inspiration Connors gave to his fans cannot be measured in matches won.

Jimmy Connors won five matches in the tournament and excited the crowd with his stirring play and repartee with the crowd and television cameras. In two of his matches against Patrick McEnroe in the first round and against Aaron Krickstein in the fourth round, Connors won in five sets where thirty-nine-year-olds were not supposed to last five sets. In the first match against Patrick McEnroe, Connors lost the first two sets, and the fans anticipated an early exit. Suddenly, Jimmy found his backhand. He roared back, pumping his fist, and the fans roared with him. He finally won the match after 1:00 a.m. in the morning.

Connors won the Krickstein match on Labor Day and on his thirty-ninth birthday after being down two sets to one and appearing to be injured in the fourth set. Sports writer Mike Lupica wrote after the match, "The match was over, but it wasn't over. True champions like Connors have a reserve of energy that they can call upon when they have nothing left."

Jimmy Connors had a great influence on the American sporting scene for two reasons. His energetic playing style, combined with his thespian antics with the crowd, increased interest in tennis enormously. He was not the greatest player ever, but like Arnold Palmer in golf, he made tennis a true American game. He made the sporting public roar like they did for Jordan in basketball and for Ali in boxing.

Connors is such a positive role model for baby boomer athletes like myself. All of us weekend athletes who play softball, tennis, touch football, golf, etc., for the love of the game can smile when they think of Connors. Jimmy was in the top ten for an unprecedented sixteen years. He has plenty of money. It's obvious he played so long because he had passion for the game and the fight. Having passion for our games, our work, and our personal life is what makes life worth living.

Women and Handicapped Athletes

The best thing about sports in the last thirty years has been the growth of women's sports at all levels and the institution of the Special Olympics for the handicapped. Women have many more opportunities to compete in all sports. The Special Olympics is a worldwide phenomenon. The handicapped compete in all age groups. We have opened up the pursuit of happiness in athletic competitions to many more people, and we should be proud.

The growth of women's sports exploded with the passage of Title IX of the Educational Amendments Act of 1972. Title IX, in effect, simply outlawed any sexual discrimination by school districts and institutions of higher education that received federal aid. Even with Title IX, the AIAW (Association of Intercollegiate Athletics for Women) initially opposed athletic scholarships.

However, when a female athlete in 1973 won a court case against the AIAW in which she charged the association with discrimination, the

AIAW quickly changed their tune. The availability of scholarships firmly launched women's sports into the mainstream of big-time intercollegiate athletics.

With Title IX, women become equal citizens in the athletic sphere of high schools, colleges, even Little League. Women in sports were everywhere. They have had a chance to develop physical, social, and leadership skills on the field. Where there was no opportunity for females, girls were allowed on boys' teams, like the Little League. A few incidents of women on boys' teams may have caused some problems. However, the overall effect has been wonderful. Girls with athletic talent now have the opportunity to develop their skills in full accord with the American dream.

When I was growing up in the 1960s, handicapped children were segregated from the world. If they were not placed in institutions, they were in special classes in schools. Athletic opportunities were nonexistent. However, we suddenly realized that the handicapped could become productive members of mainstream society. We started integrating them more with the nonhandicapped. The result has been good for everyone concerned.

Pro Sports are too Expensive and College Sports are a Better Deal

As a lifelong sports fan, I find myself moving away from pro sports and getting more interested in college and amateur sports.

When I was a kid, the top box seat at Yankee Stadium cost $4.50. Now, it costs more than $1,000, and I am not that old. Ticket prices for the top sporting events have gone up much faster than our incomes have. Most of the best seats at the major sporting events are reserved for corporations. Beers at Yankee Stadium cost more than $10, and hot dogs cost more than $5.

The conversation about pro sports is more often than not a conversation about contracts and money rather than achievement. The average fan is concerned about the financial situation of their family and not the financial situation of pro athletes. The average fan cannot relate to the financial situation of Tom Brady or Lebron James.

As a lifelong Yankee fan, I have read biographies about Mickey Mantle and Roger Maris. I also have read a biography about Derek Jeter. The books about Mantle and Maris were stories about a time when money was not all consuming and the books were very enjoyable to me. The book about Jeter was not as enjoyable to me because too many chapters of the book were focused on salary.

It just seems wrong that pro athletes are paid millions while families have to seriously budget to go to a pro game. It's a drag when I have to pay another $10 or $15 more for a ticket so a mediocre player can earn another million dollars a year that he really hasn't earned.

While semipro and college athletes don't have the skill of pro athletes, there are several advantages to following them rather than following pro athletes in person. First of all, the cost is a lot less for the ticket, food, parking, and souvenirs. Second, you usually don't have to travel as far to the game. Third, there is usually more spirit at a college game.

I am not saying to totally abandon pro sports. Fans are hooked on pro teams and athletes from their youth. Just go to pro games less and watch them on TV. This will give you more money, more time, and less aggravation when getting out of a pro stadium.

Steroids Are Worse

The recent commotion over steroid use is deserved. We should do whatever we can to address the issue. No individual is a perfect role model but harmful steroid use needs to be addressed.

Players have always tried to enhance their performance by legal or illegal means. Babe Ruth used to eat more hot dogs to try to hit farther. Some pitchers tried to throw spitballs even after they were outlawed. However, the use of steroids to enhance performance today is more dangerous than any prior means to enhance performance.

The use of steroids is more dangerous for the following reasons:

First of all, they raise an unfair advantage when one player has access to performance-enhancing drugs and others don't have this access. Ideally, the only difference in performance should be from different God-given abilities and different preparation.

Second, though steroids may enhance performance in the present for some people, they may have bad present and bad long-range effects.

Steroids could be especially damaging to young athletes, like high school athletes who are not yet fully developed.

A young high school pitcher in Texas died from drug abuse. He was a good player to begin with, good looking and popular with his classmates, but it wasn't enough. The lure of a better performance and a possible major league career was too much to pass up. Lyle Alzado, a professional football player with the Oakland Raiders, died from steroid abuse in his late thirties. To his credit, he went on TV before he passed away, to urge young athletes not to use drugs.

Third, steroids are illegal. It is not a good policy to condone the use of an illegal substance with a mere slap on the wrist. In addition, we don't want to encourage young men and women to break laws just because our athletic heroes are getting away with it. Steroid use is against the law, period. In addition, using illegal steroids can lead to other types of illegal activities.

Finally, other types of non-exemplary behavior exhibited by athletes, on and off the field, do not have the all-consuming problem of steroids. If an athlete drinks or smokes, he is being a bad role model and may endanger his health. However, he is not getting an unfair advantage over an opponent. If a player uses a corked bat or other illegal equipment, he is trying to get an unfair advantage in the game. However, no health risk is generated to the guilty player and the effect on young players is negligible.

Great Role Models

You read so much about what is wrong in sports. I would like to write briefly about who I think are three great role models in sports—Derek Jeter (baseball), Tim Tebow (football), and Mike "Coach K" Krzyzewski (basketball).

Derek Jeter

Derek Jeter was the shortstop for the New York Yankees for many years. He is now retired but his legacy lives on. I might be prejudiced because Derek played for the Yankees, and no team has media scrutiny like the Yankees have. I follow the Yankees closely, and I have never seen anything badly written about him as a player or now as an Executive and Part-Owner of the Miami Marlins.

He was not a home-run hitter in the tradition of Ruth, Gehrig, DiMaggio, Mantle, and Jackson, but he was everything else. He was the captain of the Yankees. He had three thousand career hits (a fantastic achievement) and anchored a team at shortstop that won five world championships. He hustled all the time, and he was one of the smartest players in the game. His heads-up backing up on an errant throw once turned a game around and turned a playoff series around. Also, he played in the heart of the steroid era without a hint of suspicion of his ever-taking steroids.

Derek is currently retired as a player and is an Executive with the Miami Marlins. He was recently voted into the Baseball Hall of Fame-an appropriate honor for such a great role model.

Tim Tebow

Tim Tebow is a former quarterback of the New York Jets and the Denver Broncos. He is currently an analyst for SEC Sports. Tim was a Heisman Trophy winner with Florida State. He frequently visits hospitals to cheer people up. After the Broncos defeated the Steelers in a playoff game, he visited a hospital to comfort a sick young girl. He said he was just as excited about helping the young girl as winning the playoff game.

Tim wears his heart on his sleeve and openly displayed his Christian beliefs on the football field on many occasions. Some people are turned off by his open display of thanksgiving and respect to God. However, no one can argue with the good works and positive things that Tim has done for people. He not only talks the talk, but he also walks the walk.

Coach K

Mike "Coach K" Krzyzewski is the head coach of the Duke University men's basketball team. He has coached the US Olympic team to a gold medal, and his teams have won four national championships. Coach K is also an author and inspirational speaker. Most importantly, he is regarded as a great teacher and is respected as one of the great basketball coaches of all time.

Coach K came from modest circumstances and has never forgotten where he came from. His mother cleaned floors to help support her family. Coach K emphasizes the importance of education and teamwork to his players at Duke. He refused a chance to coach in the pros for more money so he could stay at Duke to help shape young lives. Some people don't like Duke because of its elite status. One thing is sure: Duke has an elite coach.

Introduction to Personal Essays

There are six personal essays in this section. The two essays on childhood experiences are nostalgic and concern how some things were better when I was a child. The essay on time is intended to try to explain why time seems to speed up as we age and not to worry about it. The final three essays concern how we can improve the world for children as well as troubled adults.

Personal Essays

- We Had More Fun When I Was a Kid, Part I
- We Had More Fun When I Was a Kid, Part II
- Why Time Speeds Up as We Age
- Freedom of Speech and Tolerance
- Lesson from Bridgegate
- Self Esteem

Summer Was More Fun When I Was A Kid, Part I

Although we had smaller baseball gloves and only one type of sneaker for all sports, we had more fun than the kids do today. I grew up in the late 1950s and 1960s in a suburb of New York City called Garfield, New Jersey. When school was out, we had fun. We didn't have to worry about computer time. There were no computers. We didn't have to worry about a soccer practice at ten, lunch at twelve, then baseball practice at one. Our time was our own. It wasn't micromanaged like kids' time is today. Obtaining money was not the compulsion that it is today.

When we got up in the morning, we would head down to the Belmont Oval. This was an empty field in the neighborhood where we had a backstop on one end with an informal diamond. There were brush and railroad tracks on the other end. The brush and railroad tracks were far away enough so that they could not be reached except by a mighty blow.

There was a Little League in town, but the best players in the neighborhood would rather play at the oval. It was more fun. We picked our own sides by having the two captains grab a bat. You alternated hand placement going up the bat. Whoever was able to grab the top of the bat got first pick of players.

In the afternoon, there was plenty more to do. We could play another baseball game. Also, we could go exploring. We could go up to Number 8 School and play some stickball with a rubber ball. If it was really hot, we could take a dip in the pool in our backyard. We could go buy some baseball cards either at Cahayla's, Paponchak's, Elsie's, or my uncle's store—all within easy walking distance in the neighborhood. My uncle used to let me take whatever pennies I needed for my penny coin book from his store. Finding an old penny was as thrilling as getting a Mickey Mantle baseball card. If we felt like playing a game, we would flip baseball cards in our garage, play Life in our cellar, or Clue on the Hughes' patio.

Nighttime brought more activities. We would talk in front of the house. We would talk about Roger and Mickey and how the Yankees were doing. We could listen to the games on our transistor radios. When we went inside for the night, we had the option of several good shows. If the Yanks weren't on TV, we could watch roller derby or wrestling. If no sports were on, we could watch *My Three Sons*, *Leave It to Beaver*, *Bonanza*, or several other great shows. If we wanted the best scary show there ever was, we would watch *Twilight Zone*. Stephen King had nothing on Rod Serling.

In conclusion, life was full and you appreciated everything. We had recreation all day long and cool shows on TV at night. All we needed were a baseball glove and a bat, 5¢ for a pack of baseball cards, and $1 for the movies on Saturday night to be happy.

There was no constant media blitz telling us what we didn't have. When there was advertising, we rarely listened. We didn't listen because we didn't have to listen. We had everything. We had the magic of summer through a child's eyes in a more innocent time.

We Had More Fun When I Was A Kid, Part II

When I was a kid, we played pickup games all year round—baseball, stickball, touch football, basketball, and other recreational activities. We made our own rules, chose our own sides, and played in the nearest park. Now, most fields are locked up. Anytime you want some organized recreational activity, you have to worry about insurance and getting permits for fields. If you let kids be kids, they don't care about lawsuits or permits. We didn't need permits because if someone was on our field, we challenged them or just found another field. Sure, there were arguments and an occasional fight, but we had the common sense to stay away from the field bully.

In addition, we did not want parents involved in our activities. No one wanted to play with the kid whose mother was involved. That's how most mothers felt as well. Go outside and find something to do and don't come back until supper time was a frequent refrain from moms. Kids also understood how busy their moms were in running the household. This is not saying that mothers were not supportive. They were supportive of our rights to liberty and self-responsibility. They recognized the steps necessary to becoming responsible adults.

I had everything growing up in my hometown of Garfield, NJ. We had four candy stores within walking distance. You could buy anything you needed including candy, soda, baseball cards, rubber balls, and deli sandwiches. We also had Cahaylas with a pinball machine and a nickel jute box All stores were super useful Now, you have to go to another city to find four useful stores.

We also had a department store a little further away but still walkable- Two Guys. At Two Guys, you could buy clothes for all seasons, sporting goods, food, candy, records, and play pinball machines. You could also get a slice of pizza at Barcelona's on the way to Two Guys. It was never that crowded like Walmart in Garfield always seems to be.

It's no wonder that there is a children's obesity problem in this country. Too many kids just text or surf the net on their free time. With so many electronic distractions, too many kids forget to exercise and develop socialization skills. When we wanted something to do, we would meet at Cahayla's and go to a movie, go ice-skating or play some games, or go for ice cream with our friends. We were active, not talking on the phone, texting, or staring at a monitor. Doing things with your friends is more fun than staring at a monitor. Technology is great, but it does not take the place of meaningful human contact.

What's nice to know is that I think we are starting to get it. The NFL's Play 60 program is wonderful. The goal is to get children to exercise sixty minutes per day. School systems are starting to realize that eliminating physical education is a bad idea. Parents are beginning to put a limit on a child's computer and TV time. A well-rounded child, just like a well-rounded adult, can have everything today as long as they put everything in proper balance.

Why Time Seems to Speed Up as We Age and What To Do About It

As we age, time seems to speed up. The weeks seem to fly by, and one season seems to run into another. When we were younger, summers used to last for a long time. A poet once said, "To a child, a summer day lasts forever." Now, summers seem to go faster, and before you know it, we are reaching for our fall and winter clothes.

Time goes faster as we age because we build up a larger and larger memory bank every year. When we are in grammar school, a year seems more memorable because we have less to compare it against. At the age of, say, twelve, you may only remember six previous summers and two years in Little League. If you have a good summer vacation and a good year in Little League when you are twelve, the year shines in your memory as you hit the age of thirteen.

As you hit college and beyond, you may have a great year, but a lot of other things have gone on in your life so the year quickly becomes blurred. As you hit your forties, fifties, and beyond, each year seems like a blur because so much has happened in your life. Understandably, it is hard to remember how good a year five years ago was for you.

Goals

What one needs to do as one gets older is to remember that the year coming up is just as important to you as junior year in high school was to you. You can be just as happy as you were then if you take care of yourself and create meaningful goals for the current year. If there are some things you can't do anymore, like playing singles tennis, there are other just as challenging things for you, like being a good doubles player.

If next year, you don't remember what your goals were this year, so what! You know that what you did was meaningful to you at the time, and that's what makes life beautiful. Your maker put you here to live a meaningful life, so get to it.

Working towards goals and achieving meaningful steps has always made me satisfied and happy. However, working towards goals is not always enough. Sometimes, you don't achieve your goals for whatever reason. Someone won a starting position on a team instead of you. After studying long, long hours for a test, you still did not achieve the grade you wanted. Someone else married the girl or guy you were in love with at the time.

If the goal is not achievable for whatever reason, you have to find new goals. Don't dwell on the past. The World has an unlimited amount of opportunity to achieve meaningful goals and happiness.

Freedom of Speech and Tolerance

The First Amendment of the Constitution gives people the right of Freedom of Speech. It protects people of all political viewpoints. It protects the Ku Klux Klan members as well as members of the Communist Party. It also implies that we should be tolerant of all viewpoints. Unfortunately, the media, politicians, and schools don't play up this point.

When schools teach Civics and American History, they need to tie their curriculum to the need to be tolerant of all viewpoints. They need to associate learning about the First Amendment with tolerance of all viewpoints. Instead of just showing videos of marches and clashes with police, teachers need to have a lesson on tolerance and listening to all viewpoints.

If children are taught in school about tolerance, they would learn more about listening to the views of others and the need to compromise. Confrontation and assaults play up well in video excitement but bitter confrontation was not the purpose of the Founding Fathers as the means of resolving disputes. If students are taught this point early in life, they would be less drawn to extremism like the KKK or ISIS.

Lesson from Bridgegate

On May 7, 2020, the US Supreme Court threw out the convictions of Bridget Anne Kelley and Bill Baroni under wire fraud laws for realigning the access lanes to the George Washington Bridge from Fort Lee, NJ. Common Sense prevailed in this decision.

There is no doubt this was a stupid and cowardly act that inconvenienced people for days. The action was done as an act of political retribution against the mayor of Fort Lee for not supporting Governor Christie in his re-election bid. The US Attorney filed charges against them under wire fraud laws in Federal District Court. The action carried a sentence of seven years if found guilty.

No one died and there was no property changing hands as a result of this action. Nonetheless, The US Attorney won convictions in Federal District Court and US Appeals Court. Kelley and Baroni appealed the convictions for five years and the case reached the US Supreme Court which ultimately ruled in their favor.

Writing for the US Supreme Court, Justice Elizabeth Kagen said the following: "Because the scheme here did not involve money or property, Baroni and Kelly could not have violated the federal program fraud or wire fraud laws."

The Common-Sense decision in this case can be applied to lawyers and non-lawyers alike Most legal actions are justified. However, many lawyers file frivolous lawsuits trying to advance their pocketbooks or stature.

This lawsuit with a seven-year prison term was not justified according to the Supreme Court. As far as everyone else is concerned, don't knock people down without a very good reason. You don't raise yourself up by knocking someone else down.

Self Esteem

We have had way too many senseless killings lately. We also have too many suicides especially teen suicides when lives are just getting started. If you read the following, maybe it could help someone you know who is having problems.

Self Esteem*-Your overall evaluation of your worth as a person based on all the positive and negative self-perceptions that make up your self- concept.*

PARENTS WITH YOUNG CHILDREN SEEM TO HAVE MORE SELF ESTEEM IN THEIR MEANINGFUL PURSUIT OF CAREGIVING

Your self-esteem will improve if you get involved in worthwhile work and school activities including sports, special projects, and educational achievements.

People who are happy and confident with their job have higher self-esteem regardless of what the job entails. It's all about taking pride in your work.

If you know someone with low self-esteem, encourage them to join positive groups, Get a new job or learn something useful. This will raise their self-esteem. Most maniacs like Lee Harvey Oswald who killed President Kennedy had no job, no family, and no achievements.

Appendix

The following appendix contains some useful information on the topics presented in this book.

The first topic is a listing of the Amendments to the US Constitution. All of us can benefit from refreshing our knowledge of the rights we have as American citizens.

The second topic is a history of US money. It is interesting to note how the US money history has evolved from an imitation of the European system to the most sophisticated monetary system in the world.

The third topic is a listing of the ten greatest baseball achievements in one season as determined from an ESPN survey.

Amendments of the Constitution of the United States

The first ten amendments are called the Bill of Rights

I.	Freedom of religion, speech, the press, and assembly.
II.	Right to keep and bear arms.
III.	Limitation on quartering of soldiers in private homes.
IV.	Limitation on searches and seizures.
V.	Protection of personal and property rights.
VI.	Right to speedy, public, and fair trial
VII.	Trial by jury in civil cases.
VIII.	Excessive bail and cruel punishments prohibited.
IX.	People possess other rights besides those enumerated.
X.	Undelegated powers belong to the states or to the people.
XI.	Exemption of states from suit by citizens of other states.
XII.	Election of President (supersedes part of Article II, sec. 1).
XIII.	Slavery prohibited.
XIV.	Definition of citizenship. Guarantees of due process of law and equal protection of the laws against infringement by States. Constitutional adjustments to post Civil War conditions.
XV.	Right of Adult Male Citizens to Vote.
XVI.	Congress empowered to impose an income tax.
XVII.	Popular election of United States senators.
XVIII.	Prohibition of intoxicating liquors for beverage purposes.
XIX.	Right of Women to Vote.
XX.	Change in congressional and Presidential terms. Abolition of the "lame duck" session of Congress.
XXI.	Repeal of the Eighteenth Amendment.
XXII.	Limitation of President's term of office.
XXIII.	Presidential vote for District of Colombia.
XXIV.	Poll tax prohibited in election of national officers.
XXV.	Vice-President to become Acting President when President is unable to perform his duties.
XXVI.	Suffrage extended to eighteen-year-olds in both state and national elections.

Economic History of the United States

1690. Colonial Notes

In the early days of this nation, before and just after the American Revolution, Americans used English, Spanish, and French currencies. The Massachusetts Bay Colony issued the first paper money in the colonies that would later form the United States.

1775. Continental Currency

American colonists issued paper currency for the Continental Congress to finance the Revolutionary War. The notes were backed by the *anticipation* of tax revenues. Without solid backing and because they were easily counterfeited, the notes quickly became devalued, giving rise to the phrase "not worth a Continental."

1781. The Nation's First Bank

The Continental Congress chartered the Bank of North America in Philadelphia as the nation's first *real* bank to give further financial support to the Revolutionary War.

1785. The Dollar

The Continental Congress adopted the dollar as the unit for national currency. At that time, private bank-note companies printed a variety of notes.

1789

After adoption of the Constitution in 1789, Congress chartered the First Bank of the United States and authorized it to issue paper bank notes to eliminate confusion and simplify trade. The bank served as the US. Treasury's fiscal agent, thus performing the first central bank function.

1792. US Mint

The first monetary system was established with the creation of the US Mint in Philadelphia. The first American coins were struck in 1793.

1816. Second US Bank

The second bank of the United States was granted a twenty-year charter.

1836. State Bank Notes

With minimum regulation, a proliferation of 1,600 state-chartered private banks issued paper money. State bank notes with over thirty thousand varieties of color and design were easily counterfeited, which combined with bank failures to cause confusion and circulation problems.

1861. Civil War

On the brink of bankruptcy and pressed to finance the Civil War, Congress authorized the United States Treasury to issue paper money for the first time in the form of non-interest-bearing treasury notes, called Demand Notes.

1862. Greenbacks

Demand Notes were replaced by United States Notes. Commonly called greenbacks because of the green tint introduced to discourage photographic counterfeiting, they were last issued in 1971. The secretary of the treasury was empowered by Congress to have notes engraved and printed by private bank companies.

1863. The Design

The design of US currency incorporated a treasury seal, the fine-line engraving necessary for the difficult-to-counterfeit intaglio printing, intricate geometric lathework patterns, and distinctive cotton and linen paper with embedded red and blue fibers.

1865. Gold Certificates

Gold certificates were issued by the Department of the Treasury against gold coins and bullion deposits and were circulated until 1933.

The Department of the Treasury established the United States Secret Service to control counterfeiting. At that time, one-third of all circulating currency was estimated to be counterfeit.

1866. National Bank Notes

National Bank Notes, backed by US government securities, became predominant. By this time, 75 percent of bank deposits were held by nationally chartered banks. As state banknotes were replaced, the value of currency stabilized for a time.

1877. Bureau of Engraving and Printing

The Department of the Treasury's Bureau of Engraving and Printing started printing all US currencies.

1878. Silver Certificates

The Department of Treasury was authorized to issue Silver Certificates in exchange for silver dollars. The last issue was in the series 1957.

1913. Federal Reserve Act

After the 1893 and 1907 financial panics, the Federal Reserve Act of 1913 was passed. It created the Federal Reserve System as the nation's central bank to regulate the flow of money and credit for economic stability and growth. The system was authorized to issue Federal Reserve notes. Now the only US currency produced, Federal Reserve notes represent 99 percent of all currencies in circulation.

1929. Standardized Design

Currency was reduced in size by 25 percent, and a consistent design was introduced with uniform portraits on the front and emblems and monuments on the back.

1957. "In God We Trust"

Paper currency was first introduced with the inscription "In God We Trust" in 1957. The inscription appears on all currency series 1963 and later.

1990. "Security Thread and Microprinting"

Security thread and microprinting were introduced, first in $50 and $100 notes, to deter counterfeiting by advanced copiers and printers.

1999–2008. First State Quarters Collection

The mint prints a distinctive state quarter for each state, beginning with Delaware, the first state, and ending with Hawaii.

2007–2016. Presidential Dollars Collection

A distinctive gold dollar is printed for each president of the United States.

Baseball's-Ten Greatest Achievements in a Season (As Ranked from a Poll of Fans by Espn)

- *Joe DiMaggio's 56 game hitting streak in 1941.*
- *Ted Williams' .406 batting average in 1941.*
- *Hack Wilson's 191 RBI's in 1931.*
- *Nolan Ryan's 383 strikeouts in 1973.*
- *Ricky Henderson's 130 stolen bases in 1982.*
- *Denny McLain's 31 wins in 1968.*
- *Bob Gibson's 1.12 ERA in 1968.*
- *Ichiro Suzuki's 262 hits in 2004.*
- *Barry Bonds' 73 home runs in 2001*
- *Francisco Rodriguez' 62 saves in 2008*

Babe Ruth is not on this list. However, many people including myself consider the Babe the greatest baseball player ever because of his hitting and pitching prowess. The Babe hit 60 home runs in 1927-a unheard of achievement at the time when many teams did not hit 60 home runs in total. In 1917, the Babe went 23-12 with a 1.75 ERA in pitching 41 games.